feather

&

fire

poems

Cynthia
Leslie-Bole

Karen Mireau Books
Sonoma · California

ISBN: 978-1-968822-00-2

Cover photo:
with thanks to Todd Pickering
toddpickering.com

for my mother
Miriam Bennett Leslie
October 22, 1930 - October 21, 2024

Birthday

we lay you down
beneath the mountain's gaze
in a meadow of wildflowers

moss cradles you
with a mother's touch
on your time-worn skin

columbine
larkspur and
shooting stars
crown your silver head

your life flows away
with the snow-fed stream

your body melts
into metamorphic ground

your spirit takes wing
in the sun-warmed breeze

Petition to Uriel

angel of
expression
and wisdom

please help me
convey a true thing
touch a true heart
utter a true word

at least once

Contents

Lineage of Loss

Finding / Losing / Finding

Incubation

SCAFFOLDING

Who Can Argue
with a Mountain?

feel me, poet
feel the density, the depth, the gravity
of my incalculable tonnage
no downward boundary or
separate self distinguishable
from earth's molten core
that warms me from below
as rarified winds tickle my peaks

I harbor ever-changing life forms and elements
yet have my own deep solidity and a subsonic voice
like the guttural rumble of time itself
I witness, I testify, I stand
for essential truths and tangible hereness

you cannot argue with me
my unassailable existence always prevails
my immensity dwarfs metaphors and machinations
of humans who poetize on my flanks
like fruit flies humming on an over-ripe fig

go ahead, use me as you will
find your nourishment, your inspiration
but be prepared to be startled
by the brute reality of me:

the flash flood that carries you away
before you perfect your sentence
the lightning that zaps your precious pen
and turns you to cinders
the earthquake that shakes your bones
and sends your fragile pages
scattering in the winds

Scaffolding

one strand of spider silk
stretched from oak to oak
shimmers with sun spectra
shivers above leaf leather

a thread
thinner than breath
lighter than thought
holding the trees erect

I bow my head
and duck under it
honoring the architecture
from which the woodland is woven

Beguilement

poison oak

freshest leaves
in the spring woods

a pale-pink bridal blush
translucent with sunlight
thin as my sensitive skin

just asking

to be touched

California Buckeye

in winter your branches point and twist
like Dickensian fingers
your bark the steely color of apocalypse

but what's this?

pointed buds at the end of slender twigs?

then buds opening into fanfares of lacy flowers?

soft scents wafting into spring air
and nectar inviting bees to a Dionysian feast?

please forgive me for my mistake
sweet neighbor

February Orchestra

streams trickle
a melody over rocks

frogs chirp
from fresh mud

owls call basso and soprano
across the woodlands

wind whistles
through finely-tuned canyons

and though I can't hear it
I'm sure

fungi hum
through their gills

while moss strums
the cool air with feathery fingers

just because
that's what they do

in February

Crow's Message

small songbirds defer to the fat, sleek crow
who feeds on seeds dropped in the rush to fill bellies
dwarfing finches, juncos, chickadees
who are the intended recipients

crow
so glorious and raucous
impervious to the drizzle
that sheens her already glossed feathers
so unbothered by others' opinions
about decorum, right speech, and rules

crow
who enters the world fully voiced
never muting herself
or trying to be anything other than
the personality-rich puzzler
curious troublemaker
proud preener and strutter
she came here to be

tiny birds make themselves scarce
ceding their seed with respect
for this avian higher power
this wiser cousin whose presence
seems strong as the wind itself

crow
in the green, misted morning
commands me through the window:

See my body.
It is beautiful and I know it.
Hear my voice.
It cuts through the noise and I use it.
Behold my wings. They are vast in this small yard
and I spread them wide as the sky
with joy.

Laughingstock

I was made a laughingstock
by a pair of jays today

I heard the guttural gurgles of crow
then the piercing cries of red-tail hawk

I looked up and there they were
two stellar jays perfecting their mimicry
bouncing branch to branch, flexing their crowns
and flicking their tails with the sheer fun of it all

I laughed along with them like a happy fool
while great horned owls hooted love songs
to each other through the oaks

Hummingbird Medicine

even hummingbird
dancer of joy
flasher of jewels
defender of sweetness
needs to rest sometimes

there is no apology in this

sometimes she must close her eyes
to the riot of color that nourishes her

sometimes she must cease
zoom and buzz
delight and dazzle
to restore her flaming vitality

she locks feet around a twig
slows metabolism, heartbeat, breath
and surrenders to restorative torpor

and there she rests until
sun kisses her feathers
lifeforce surges
wings flare open
and nectar again
fills her belly
in the simple cycle
of surging then ebbing
swooping then sleeping
radiant throughout

Bird Watching Taxonomy

Are you a
Cooper's Hawk
or a
Sharp-shinned Hawk?

Neither.

I
    am
        myself

   and
    you
       could
          never
            pronounce
           my
             name.

One Particular Bird

I call *hey, birdie birdie*, and a scrub jay comes
black eyes gleaming, moving closer in staccato hops
head cocking in curiosity

she sits above me, starts to sing, not squawk
crooning a closed-beak lullaby
melodies, trills, rumbles ascending and descending
so quiet I can hear only because I am inches from
her curved belly, her ruffling throat
she is courting, soothing, singing of spring

she spies the peanut
hops to my hand, bows, grasps with black beak
flies to a loftier branch
tap-tap-tapping to shatter the shell, ingest nourishment
letting peanut confetti flutter to flagstones below

she doesn't fly away, she stays
we relax together, nowhere to go
enjoying new leaves exploding on the pistache tree
and blossoms burgeoning on the dogwood

just two beings hearing crows
harass a red-shouldered hawk
glad the commotion has nothing to do with us

On Tomales Bay

boats drift on the mirror catching morning light
seals observe with dog-eyed curiosity
limestone cliffs shine bone-like
in a ghost-town gulch

long-beaked loons wail mournful calls
otters corkscrew like children of sea
cormorants white-wash islands with guano
clouds brush blue sky with fragile calligraphy

cypress trees let air sculpt their hair
tuxedoed buffleheads suavely court beloveds
herons balance on stick-legs waiting to spear
neon kayaks slice the still surface

surf scoters whistle their wings while taking off
pelicans dive in the brine to fill lunch-bucket gullets
while elk with lethal antlers
choose the peace of browsing

Of Love and Loneliness

one little brown bat
(common name)
also known as Myotis lucifugus
(scientific name)
who is one-inch long, furred in taupe suede
and sporting round ears of fragile leather
nests under my deck

I first spied the scat of this flittermouse
(Old English name)
on the kayak beneath where he cozies up
between joists during the day

upon first viewing, he became to me Bernie Sanders
(given name)
although perhaps he should have been My Otis
(punning name)
and I loved him as a mother loves any small, soft creature

my joy, however, was tempered
with concern that first summer
because one bat does not a colony make
and loneliness seemed to cloak Bernie in further shadow
as he slept solo under the deck

but the next summer—glad tidings—there were two:
Bernie and Bernadette
(or perhaps Bernie and Bernardo)
and I sighed contented, knowing my small friend
had found another of his ilk

this summer, though, the pile of droppings
diminished by half
and now Bernie is again hanging alone by his tiny toes
while I fret about white-nose fungus that may extirpate
(oh evil word)
all little brown bats within twelve years

I know the lifespan of Myotis lucifugus
is often well beyond ten years, so now I have to worry
that Bernie may live long enough
to be the last little brown bat in the world
hanging all by himself beneath my deck
while a little brown bit of me
pines away to nothing as well

PATTERN
LANGUAGE

Connective Tissue

connection
is my necessary thing
and it comes to me in details

fur coating the lupine pod
seeds on the strawberry like stars in a galaxy
sun-yellow beak jutting from the junco's black hood
gradations of purple to pink in the sweet pea blossom

sudden meeting of eyes in which someone is truly home
looking out and seeing me, who is also home,
with hearth fires burning in welcome

ivy waving in the wind
egret flying with black feet trailing behind
sticky monkeyflower sporting orange gullets
dudleya growing squat with red spires reaching high
my husband offering me cardamom tea and a smile

unrelated details yet part of the matrix
that keeps me from dispersing

connections
meeting, merging, branching, extending
and swirling me back
to our common source

Pattern Language

I find a fallen log
with serpentine routes incised into naked wood
a message written in insect hieroglyphics
a lost language of beetle and hunger

I submerge in the patterns
until they become veins snaking
rivers meandering, neuronal pathways branching

why does everything
mirror everything else?

why do
fronds
sunflowers
snails and nebula
all swirl in spirals?

why does my cat's smile
look like my husband's grin?

why do whales' transoceanic songs
reflect elephants' subsonic rumblings
that move for miles through the ground?

why does fog move like waves and waves like fog?
why do my questions seem like bark beetle wanderings?

a hawk's cry pierces my reverie and suddenly it's clear
my mind's aperture is too narrow
to admit the full spectrum
of creation's interconnected designs anyway

Forest Web

accompanied by
coolness of shade
aromas of conifers
echoes of owl calls
I step into a ring of trees

and inclusion seeps into me

in dappled forest
where generations live
in crowns of redwood royalty
I look toward the canopy

and ongoingness suffuses me

I know rushing and pushing make me stale
waiting and pacing make me unreachable
reviewing and rehearsing wall me off

but if I expand perspective
I am whisked into the web
where individual lives burgeon and ebb
in gossamer the creator makes and mends endlessly

she tells me I am safe in her silk
with all her other beloveds
and the remedy for what ails me
is to become like the oldest tree
swaying in union with earth and sky
living and dying and everything in between
without struggle or resistance

Still

a hammock hangs beneath redwoods
its colors bright and its threads strong
waiting for ones who move too fast, do too much
to enter its embrace and be still

we planted the redwoods thirty years ago
when our daughter was born
they grew above her and shaded her
then expanded further to shelter our son

the trees doubled then tripled in height
offering their branches so small humans could know
the joy of ascension in the arms of arboreal kin

until one day the familial bond was shaken
when a gardener's heedless pruning
severed the redwood's low branches
making climbing impossible

yet trees and children still grew
breaking and shedding
sprouting and reaching
stretching ever farther away
from our imagined realm of protection

now the children are grownups and elsewhere
the redwoods are giants and still here
witnessing the passage of our lives
and evolution of our loves

we practice acceptance with the trees
as we age and weather together
glad their lifespans will exceed ours

and still the hammock waits
a cocoon dreaming of a caterpillar
inviting us to rest beneath old friends
whose presence attests to shared history
and the glorious fact of mutual survival

Between Species

every day
my son's cat brings a newborn opossum
through the cat door and deposits it on the floor

and every day
my son gathers the pointy-nosed, naked-tailed babe
and puts it back in its hole under the deck
with slices of cucumber to soothe its distress

for longer than I know,
cat and man repeat these gestures of caring and carrying
as though tenderness could
save the world
soothe the children
console the mothers
celebrate the survivals
become a radical choosing
of kindness, peace, creation
over predation, violence, destruction

Bodies of Water

we are bodies of water
transforming

droplet evaporating from azalea leaf
mist dispersing from steaming sequoia
cloud eating fog, in turn being consumed by sun

spring rain plumping emerald moss
moisture fueling calypso orchid's fragile flowering

teeming vernal pool leaning toward disappearance
snow-melt stream flooding
though its source will soon be gone

amniotic ocean receding and rising, warming and changing
towards who-knows-what poignant fate

puddle dispersing into diamonds of slurry
from the stomp
of a child's red boot

PRAYER
OF THE SENSES

Of Mystery and Majesty

I want to speak the language of
rock and river
moss and mushroom
bird and beetle

I want to be an outgrowth of earth
like a mountain risen from her skin

I want to fill with sky
thoughts like clouds
breath like conversation
between leaf and lung

I want to be mystical yet clear eyed
salt on my tongue
dirt between my toes
able to hold grief, suffering and violence
within the larger embrace
of mystery and majesty

After Dining with Hyper-Rationalists

sometimes my brain doesn't want to explain
figure out, tease apart or double down

it gets fatigued from standing up for the unquantifiable
when interacting with data-driven factual folk

it wears thin on analyzing, rationalizing, theorizing
it gets sick of scrunching tight to see the light

my brain often chokes on brittle fare like
cogitate, explicate, stipulate, formulate

it prefers to sip soups with ingredients like
create, animate, elevate, illuminate

sometimes my brain rebels against compressing
into ever smaller self-reverential folds

it fears it could constrict to walnut size
then collapse inward until not even thought could escape

sometimes my brain wants to relax its wrinkled brow
stretch out and float
like a jellyfish riding the salty seas

it wants to step out of its skull
like a lady freed from her corset
and take a good, deep breath

it wants to expand like a plant
sprung loose from a too-tight pot
and reach into new fertile soil

sometimes my brain wants a sabbatical
from being laser
rather than lantern

it wants to burn like a pilot light
flaring as needed in service
to its wiser sister: the dear, kind heart
and its elder mentor: the timeless, welcoming soul

Circular Reasoning

a circle believes in centrifugal force
spinning, twirling

the power of one
indivisible, unbreakable
all points equally chosen and blessed

start anywhere, go any place
it doesn't matter
a circle has no preference
it doesn't believe in
beginning, ending, starting, finishing

a circle says
can't you see as I see?
why build lines in your mind?
why insist on forward and backward?
why squeeze time into an arrow's narrow shaft?

take as your model
the whirlpool, the tornado
the dust devils and seasonal cycles

accept as your teacher the moon
ringed with prismatic moonbows
shimmering with light
waxing and waning
without apology
or need to go
anywhere
at all

Technology as Teacher

my computer freezes
and spins the pinwheel of death
when my fingers command it to write

but then invisible hands move the cursor
pointing my attention
to nothing

and the guru in the laptop presses return
again and again
to generate space
and more
space

so whiteness can write
its own story

and blankness can sing
its silent song

I bow my head
and scribble
on a piece of paper
instead

Where Awareness Dwells

I don't want to be lost in thought
I want to be found in alertness
so I am minding my mind
pulling my awareness
from the turret on top
downstairs into the house
of organs, bones, and cells

often my mind bobs back to the surface
with upward-seeking buoyancy
desiring to commune with
words, thoughts, wonderings, ponderings
anything rather than immerse in the
slow, dense realm of physicality

but when I attend within my body
cells and systems wake up
and their response is joyous, astonished
I can feel their aliveness and desire to be included

they say:
we have much to contribute
turn down your blaring thought-radio
and hear the messages we send without words

we offer direct experience
no mental constructs needed to live, move, know
as one organism made of up myriad parts

we are the internal nebula
living, dying, birthing, withering
shining brightly, pulsing darkly

we comprise countless layers of micro and macro
so deeply intertwined as to be inseparable

we are viral, bacterial, fungal, and human
a vibrant, embodied community
where despite what your mind claims
your fundamental awareness
actually dwells

Somatic Experience

first a glassine thud
then a perishable image
that still burns bright:
towhee splayed on patio
eyes glass-black
head thrust severely back
neck surely broken
spindly legs akimbo
talons curled in death clutch

then it starts:

toes contracting, legs vibrating, torso twitching
head melting from extreme tilt
back to angle of repose
life force shuddering through stunned bird
amazed to find itself among the quick
before flying off
thoroughly resurrected

how often do I fail to notice such pivotal moments
where destiny hangs undecided
waiting languorously for a push or a passing whim
to decide thumbs up or thumbs down
regarding the fate
of an intricate
irreplaceable
bit of creation?

Different Kinds of Folks

some folks try to build up the centrifugal force
of merit and karmic cleansing
as they spin through loops of many lives
hoping to be flung free eventually
from the wheel of samsara into the bliss of nirvana

but I am a different kind of beast
one who chooses to slide belly against the ground
licking each dewdrop and
peering through grass blades
lucent in the sun

I am one who feels that my precious body and life
and all the brilliant manifestations of earth herself
are to be revered as a necessary counterbalance
to the quest for spiritual liberation

I feel no hurry to exist solely in celestial realms

I came here to be here
to be duality incarnate as a human of limited vision
and I love the whole shebang almost more than I can bear

so much for nonattachment

some folks say they came back from near-death experiences
because the afterlife is so blissfully smooth
that it lacks the friction necessary for growth

I am a devotee of growth

so let me keep looping through life in arising spirals
like a hawk riding thermals higher and higher
with ever keener and wider perspectives

let me keep loving again and again
in ever deepening pools of connection
right down to the bubbling
source of love itself

let me throw the chaos, confusion, and grief
of being human
into the crucible at earth's core
to transfigure
into something potent and elemental
that allows me to be
a praising, evolving creature dancing lightly
with the illusory scarves of samsara
through this life and beyond

Samadhi Tending

tend each other
with attention
and intention

these words move like seeds
carried on currents
from heart
to
head
to
hands

they germinate
and grow
into kindness
which fruits
into wholeness

which fertilizes
fresh reciprocal tenderness
between givers and receivers
who are in essence
one and the same

Prayer of the Senses

I would like to hear one clear note
without wondering what voice made it

I would like to smell one astonishing scent
that stops me in my tracks

I would like to see one brilliant color
without wanting to scan for more

I would like to taste one sharp spice
and let it linger on my tongue until done

I would like to feel one tender caress
as though it is the only thing
I will ever need to know

LINEAGE OF LOSS

The Conversation

I imagine keeping company with a crocodile
sitting immobile
trying not to look like enticing prey
but he doesn't care

belly round with rodent, bird, feral cat
yellow eyes heavy-lidded in the sun
teeth jutting in echo of curved claws

I am fascinated by his utter repose
and lulled by his soporific state

I sidle closer
smell his stink of fish and carrion
see the symmetry of his scales
hard as bone, smooth as polished jade

I behold the droplets of water on his snout
like diamonds bestowed by a riverine god

we are at peace together, mutually respectful
basking in creaturely communion
I want to touch him
to feel his solidity, our solidarity
so I lean in closer

his nostrils twitch
open/shut
and arrows of energy shoot my way

"Don't be a fool,"
he says
without moving a muscle

"My death, your death could come now or later.
Death is potential,
patient like a reptile waiting in the endless night.
It will come as it will,
fierce and startling, like jaws crushing a throat,
or soothing and motherly, like a soft breath
snuffing a wick-spent candle."

"*In the end,*" he says, "*it's all the same.*"

my heart rate spikes
my pulse surges through my veins

I scoot my body back through wet grass
trying not to act like prey
respectfully retreating but still mesmerized

"*I see,*"
I say
from a somewhat safer distance

his armored, muscled tail
flicks in acknowledgment

"*Just so you know,*"
he says
and closes his eyes

Deciphering the Dreams

if only I could decipher the dreams
to stop their recurrence

ones where I can't see or wake from sleep
to deal with the situation at hand

ones showing how I fail in my duties
and am unprepared for what lies ahead

ones where helpless beings are lost or in danger
(my mother/my child/my creature)
but I can't find or protect them

if only I could hang onto my babies
and confused mother
if only I could stand up for myself
and defend others
if only I could awaken
to see clearly and act competently

these dreams plague me and seem immune
to exorcism and banishment

but perhaps the dream to hold is the one where
even though blind and terrified
I drive home with dependents on board
without hitting anything or harming anybody

only later to realize
I'm sightless because I taped my own eyes shut
to test my mettle and learn self-trust

Expectations

I tried to find the extraordinary

I scrutinized the horizon
looking for the bright blur
of a once-in-a-lifetime comet
supposedly visible right beside Venus
but all I saw was a shawl of soft fog
flowing and pouring like liquid cashmere
over the silhouetted shoulders
of the Point Reyes peninsula

I searched the sky from sunset to sleep
for the dancing northern lights
recently viewed nearby
but all I saw was a crescent moon
reflecting on wave tops
like a path to illumination
then setting as a shark fin of silver
behind the black ridge

I petitioned for help for mother, daughter, self
asking for a way out of our human predicaments
but I received
no fireball streaks of epiphany
no shimmering displays of insight
no glimmers of how we three
can be soothed or saved or delivered
without struggle into whatever is next

all I got was contentment
the ability to feel our inviolable connection
and renewed resolve
to carry our shared lineage forward
as best I can

Flailing Steward

the responsibility to shepherd the dying
towards their ending is a heavy one

what is my job as steward
of the precious life of my mother?
when do I bring in hospice and stop curative attempts?

I try to intuit her soul's hidden wishes
but the messages are murky

do I heed my sweet, demented mother when she says
I'm not ready to die yet
or do I follow her request from the days of sound mind
to prioritize preserving her dignity?

does her current fierce wanting to continue
override her previous desire to depart
when quality of life becomes nil?

how I wish I knew her soul, body and mind
were working in concert to direct the appropriate ending
so I as a flailing steward
won't have to

Boat / Woman / Anchor

gray waves toss a fishing boat
tethered only to a concrete block on the bay floor
and a gyrating buoy on the surface

my own gray curls wind-whip my eyes, mouth, nostrils
making it hard for me to speak or see the far shore

I sense soil below my feet and silt beneath the boat
I try to find my footing, feel my mooring
to that which buoys me up
and keeps me from being carried away
by the currents and tidal fluxes
buffeting my small consciousness

dirt and sea spray carried in gusts brine my skin
until I am made of land and ocean
a scrim, a crust, a badge of belonging
stiffening my face and etching my wrinkles white
like a storm-tossed, salt-of-the-earth old woman

I prefer the salted crow's feet at the corners of my eyes
to the downward lines around my mouth
but I come by both honestly

and I stand as steady as I can
with feet planted and hands on hips
sending down roots
to anchor my battered, buoyant heart

Lineage of Loss

eyes watch from the other side
ancestors who remember
carrying and protecting
losing and grieving

even ancient ones who came
before those who can be traced
hold the memory of dying infants
wasting partners and
fading mothers

we know how it is
they say

we are helping you carry your griefs
just as our grandmothers helped us carry ours

this is soul-honing work
nothing to be done but open your heart
and tend through the end and beyond

there is no protecting against sorrow
no avoiding the pain of losing who you love

you will be gutted by life no matter what you do
they say

look into the immense, mysterious face of loss
and accept her as a tender guide
who connects you with all beings
and with us

Bodily Impact

after her last breath
my love-filled
love-fueled mother
becomes a body
and it hits me hard:

without her body
my body would not exist

I entered this realm
through the now-empty vessel
lying before me

she gestated my body
and the eggs that made
my children's bodies

but soon this cooling form
that housed my vibrant mother
will exist only as
atomic components
of earth's body

and my daughter body
will never
touch
her mother body
again

Facing the Sun

if I still could

I would say to my mother

I want more wildflower walks
more hiking in the Rocky Mountains
more picnicking with sublime vistas
more delighting in babies and birds
more frozen yogurt with toppings
more turning to face the sun
more spring country drives
more stories and questions
more festive celebrations
more frivolous shopping
more popcorn at movies
more ladies' luncheons
more holding hands
more belly laughs
more simple love

with you

The Cosmic Book

life and death are marbled
like the end sheets of books
swirling with gold and cobalt
intermingling in movement

stories come and go
no matter how perfectly written
to convey the dramas inside

characters come and go
no matter how richly developed
to enliven the roles they inhabit

perhaps we are all
momentary masterpieces
in the divine library

if we had a galaxy of senses
and a big-bang heart
perhaps we might grasp a bit of
the devastating beauty
and volcanic passion
that undergird creation and destruction
and marble every page of the book
that never ends

FINDING / LOSING / FINDING

Feather and Fire

a photographer lights a feather
and shoots it mid-burn

I see the image and am seared, shocked
not sure if I am viewing
sacrilege or sacrament

I carry it in my mind's eye
see the flame dancing off to the right
as though blown by a capricious breeze
rapturously consuming the bit of bird
that once knew flight

to understand
I look up feather anatomy, learn its language

calamus, downy barbs
after-feather, rachis
barbule, hooklets

as with God
words only hint at the mystery

to understand
I find my own feather, take it home
and with a profane, mundane butane lighter
torch the thing in my sink

no sacred symbol there
just keratin smell of fancified hair burning
just acrid smoke and blackened curling
with no transcendent flame

finally
to understand
I write a poem with words like
metamorphosis singing in undertones
and *transformation* soaring into open air
exalting in feathers aflame
fire and flight uniting
matter becoming airified, rarified in a new way
that sparks my heart into its own
spontaneous combustion

Morning Prayer

morning wind
bring me my breath
fresh with dew
new for this moment

let me be a zealot for joy
a fierce flame for love
an amplifier for awakening

let me trust revelations and
glimmers of goodness
as hints of abiding truth

let me bloom even in dust
like a desert orchid
powered by earth's will

let me open my mind
as a lotus of light
rooting my body
in the silt of experience

let me feel my cells' sentience
and heed their wise guidance

let me hear my own note
in the song of the universe
and sing it with my life

Finding / Losing / Finding

Act I – Water

I found it
had it for a long time
held it in my hand
cool and indigo like the deepest sea

then I lost that blazing jewel

it rolled from my palm
skittered across the beach
was consumed by the roiling surf

my clarity faded, as well as my purpose
my sense of being in the flow
of being buoyantly held

until yesterday in a sheltered cove
where waves sighed onto shore
a raft of foam delivered a different gem to me
this one smaller, more delicate
perhaps a shade lighter, a touch brighter

I wove the prize into my hair
for safekeeping
like an egg in a silver nest
to incubate, perhaps even grow
in size and brilliance
I won't rush it or crush it
with hopes and expectations

I trust the gift will find its way
into my siren's crown
someday

Act II – Earth

I used to have a seed
dark brown
polished to a high shine
big, bold, bursting with potential
carrying its own mystery
like a sly smile

I held it close
protective, proprietary
as though I could bring about its fruition
with the sheer force of my longing

but as I wandered it must have fallen
through a hole in my pocket

I mourned, I yearned
I felt my potential wither and shrivel
until I lay on the ground and surrendered

then the soil offered me a different seed
its own shade of dark chocolate
more rough than polished
more humble seeker than proud striver

I tucked the pip under my tongue
for safekeeping

the seed will be freed
when the case opens like a heart in rapture
and words of wonder
curl in tendrils from my mouth
someday

Act III – Air

I once had the smallest, brightest
hummingbird feather
dazzling symbol of freedom and flight
talisman of my teacher, the harbinger of joy

I kept my treasure in a magnifying box
where I could peer at it and keep it safe

but the lid got dusty, dimming the iridescence
so I opened the box
and my exhaled greeting lifted the feather
sending it aloft on the wind's greater breath
until it disappeared

I quickly felt gravity's weight
thud me down with leaden feet
and I lost my lift, my luster, my buzz, my zoom

until one day a sister feather appeared
as if by magic on the counter
a present perhaps from the generous breeze
blowing through my open door

now a new hummingbird's feather
rests lightly in an open bowl
I don't worry about it disappearing
on a current when I sneeze

I know the feather will fly with me
when I grow my own
small wings
someday

Yesterday's Spirals

pages upon pages in journal after journal
I read messages sent in years past
from my soul to myself

some words glow
some are bland leftovers
my pulse threads throughout

mixed with dross are delicacies
words alive and lit with knowing
phrases that still sing with revelation

digesting epiphanies from old selves
gives me compassion
for their struggles, their rehashed stories
their flashes of breakthrough into new seeing
only to forget then discover again
the view from a different elevation

it is a spiral process
with subtle gains on each rotation
through the labyrinthine life
that is mine

Timescales

time rolls in waves
cresting and crashing in tumult
then calming to a whisper again

meanwhile we squeeze ourselves
into the clocked intervals
we impose on intrinsic tempos

earth has many:
glacial time scraping and freezing
metamorphic time heating and squeezing
sedimentary time accreting and eroding
volcanic time erupting and flowing
tectonic time sliding and buckling

and there's life time
cadence of creatures and plants
birthing, seeding, evolving, vanishing
as earth turns in sun's light
and moon teases seas
into tidal undulations

sometimes
if we are still
we can glimpse
the timelessness
behind these timescales
out of which each
fresh moment
is born

Nesting Bowls

the creator holds the greater bowl
big enough to fit numberless nebulae
black holes and dark matter
bright suns and supernovas

it's a very large bowl decorated with
golden light and silver shadows
sloshing with the creamy froth of creation

the monk holds a more modest bowl
made of gourd or unglazed clay
decorated only with a hand-polish
of patience and dedication

it contains humility and reverence
and food gifted from the people
in thanks for meditation to free all beings

the child holds the diminutive bowl
encircled by grubby fingers
decorated with crayon scribbles
of visions from beyond the veil

this bowl holds untutored knowing
innocent offerings, playful possibilities
bursting into being anew every moment

she sees everything and nothing in her bowl
depending on how she looks at it
she feels gaiety and tears twinned, entwined

she tosses her bowl into the air
it falls to the ground and settles on a slant
endlessly spilling invisible contents
like a self-replenishing fountain

INCUBATION

After the Election:
Possible Ways to Respond

in the stunned, speechless silence
a question mark
purple-black as a bruise
floats untethered

don't know what the question is, but it goes deep
don't know what the answer is, but it goes wide

possible ways to respond
arise for consideration

be as the kelp
tough enough to withstand storms in swaying forests
yet supple enough to let seals pass with grace

be as the crab
built to move sideways instead of ever forward
able to scuttle for cover and
grab the good with pincer precision

be as the halibut
giving reality the side-eye, cozying into sand to disappear
while waiting to see what sustenance the current brings

or be as the fishermen
crab traps laid, lines out for halibut
patient as their prey
content to float above kelp on the moving waters
with sunlight dancing in their eyes

Post-Election Thought Experiment

in my imagination
I walk by trumpeting signs
flinch as though slapped
climb the steps
enter the stranger's home
heart fluttering, breath shallow
smile forced to convey
I mean no harm

she meets me with minted lemonade
or black tea brewed just right

we sit

she offers cookies with chocolate chunks
my favorite

we ask about husbands
inquire about livelihoods
light up telling tales of offspring

when she tells of recent mother loss
her eyes brim
my heart sighs
me too, I say with a wobble

we look at autumn color outside
leaves zigzagging in their descent

we sip, we swallow

I ask what is most important to her
she says, love and wellbeing for friends and family

she asks what is most important to me
I say, love and wellbeing for friends and family

and the earth, I add, risking divisive territory
but she nods

we munch, we swallow

we dab lips with paper napkins
I ask, would you like to discuss the situation?
she says, not really, how about you?

I say, me neither
thinking, no need to dip into our bucket
of stubborn stories

so we sit

and we listen to
ice clinking against glasses
or tea sloshing in grandmother cups
or crows in the branches cawing
about who is sleekest, blackest, best

we sit like basic human beings
unadorned by stale illusions

we sit like we belong
watching trees shed their loads
and carpet the ground
with cold fire

Topsy-Turvy

hasn't everything
always seemed topsy-turvy?
haven't we always griped
about how things were better
in the good old days?
how things are going
to hell in a handbasket?
how the only future
is apocalypse?

Neanderthals must have raged
against Homo sapiens domination
and denizens of lost civilizations
undoubtedly clung to what they cherished
but the vanquished persisted by sending DNA forward
like time capsules to seed new beings

is it not the way of change to churn like a geothermal pool
bubbling, spewing, steaming new things into being?

if we get too close to the source
we'll be scalded beyond recognition
but at just the right remove
we bear baffled witness
to forces of creation and destruction
that swirl and refract like an opal eye
with a deeper view

the eye doesn't blink or look away
because it sees dispassionately
that all is as it should be
that life remains undaunted
even if it must renounce
the world occasionally
to regroup

we cannot discern
the broad perspective
our eyes are not equipped
our minds are too small
it is not our purview
to behold what gods perceive
playing out on the cosmic stage

it has always been thus
and it seems our role is to
wail and resist while nevertheless
tumbling and spinning onward
with hopeful, fearful hearts
and fingers crossed
behind our backs
as we move into
the fertile
future

Responsiveness Prayer

give me different eyes
when the grey scale settles like a gauzy pall
over the vibrance of life

wake my heart
when its cadence turns sluggish and
compassion feels distant

show me the direction of love
when my needle spins
and true north is found only
in cave-dark silence

slap my mouth when my speech turns ugly
sucking beauty from the world
instead of raising praise

burn away my indifference
when I freeze protectively
and can't bear to see unbearable suffering

kick my feet forward
when I become too rooted
in the stasis of my own comfort and safety

guide me when I grow rigid
to become semi-permeable like a cell membrane
opening and closing in apt response
to what is truly happening

Role Model

I grope for a role model
to guide me through
uncharted terrain
and I think

what about the donkey
who knows herself
as her own strong boss?

what about her
sensitive nose
ever-swiveling ears and
curious brown eyes?

what about her
glorious switch of a tail
that can shoo flies
from the face of a friend?

what about her
ability to withstand heat
go without water and
eat coarse vegetation
most animals can't digest?

what about her
calm disposition
keen intelligence
good memory and
problem-solving skills?

what about her
sharp-hooved kick
her sturdiness and steadiness
carrying the load that
is hers to carry?

Relief

when the world feels too big
go small

trace a snail's trail
glistening through grass

deliver a sunbaked earthworm
back to its black-soil haven

let an ant march across your finger
risking the bite that will wake you

study a scarlet pimpernel
in the wilderness of your lawn

move to the cadence of sequoias
practicing the slow grow

apprentice to a spider thread
luminous in the sun

locate your still point under
a fairy-pink mushroom

find the temple of relief
hiding right here

in the small

Incubation

we can stare at
the incubating egg
tap its creamy curve
press our ear to its shell
or demand it explain itself
but still we cannot know
what grows inside

we can check the almanac
about patterns of hatching
sit on the white mystery
with our own warm bottoms
or try to hasten the reveal
by singing a birth song
but still we cannot know
what will emerge

it could be a dinosaur
who grows to rapacious size
and tears the flesh of the world

it could be a hummingbird
who delights with acrobatics
and flashes of ruby brilliance

it could be a platypus
who defies mammalian norms
by wrapping offspring in shells

it could be an ouroboros
who swallows its tail
in ever-renewing cycles

or it could be our own potential
curled tight and waiting for
the right conditions to emerge

whatever the contents
eventually the egg tooth
will rip or crack its case

whatever the creature
it will one day be ready
to break free and meet
its destiny

but for now
not knowing is intimacy
patience is respect
and tending is ritual
as we prepare for
the something new
that wants to
break through

Regarding Translucence

how can a spring leaf be so luminous?

I know
I know

the sun shines through it
making it glow

but it seems to be more than that

it seems the leaf is radiant
with the fire of life itself

alight with the
ecstasy of becoming

offering me a glimpse
of another way to be

After All

after all this living
convictions crumble
illusions dissipate
philosophies disintegrate
into wisps and tatters
that I weave into a soft nest
in which to rest

I sense a new
earth-filled, body-felt magic
sprouting from spirit's generous hand
emptiness and fullness moving as they will
through the pith of my heart

my prayers become smoke
earth's dreams become blossoms
fierceness mellows into love
and finally
I am able to meet you
somewhere true

ACKNOWLEDGMENTS

With endless gratitude
to my family:

Ben, my heart;
Haley and *Holden*, my blood;
Mimi and *Don*, my bones; and
Faye and *Caroline* for enriching my life,
expanding my family, and supporting my offspring.

With thanks to my teachers
on the embodied spiritual journey:

Adam Baraz
Jane Brunette
Kerry Brady
George and Georgia Bertelstein
Erika Campbell Wright
Arkan Lushwalla
Margarita Loinaz
Carmen Hering
Dawn Averitt
Cathy Whyte

With deep appreciation
to my soul sisters:

Sally Bolger, treasured partner on the path and writing buddy who devoted endless hours to helping me polish this collection;

Karen Mireau, most generous friend and literary midwife who helped me birth this book into physical form;

Jane Brunette, writing and soul-work guide extraordinaire in whose group most of these poems began;

Shari Bashin-Sullivan, who provides the daily sustenance and bright spice that keep my life nourishing and delicious; and

Lissa Rovtech, with whom I have shared idiosyncrasies, joys and challenges for four delightful decades.

Cynthia Leslie-Bole

ABOUT THE AUTHOR

Cynthia Leslie-Bole is a writing coach, editor and certified writing group leader living in Orinda, California. Her work has appeared in the anthology *Fire and Rain: Ecopoetry of California,* as well as in more than twenty *Pure Slush* and *Truth Serum* anthologies and other journals.

In *The Luminous In-Between,* her first poetry collection, Cynthia explores marriage, motherhood, individuation and kinship with nature, while celebrating our capacity to create, heal and perceive what lies beyond the ordinary.

Her chapbook, *Tiny Sacraments,* traces her deepening connection with earth and spirit as she navigates loving and caring for elderly parents in the final stages of their lives.

The poems in this collection, *Feather & Fire,* encompass a period in Cynthia's life following a severe concussion, an acute heart incident poetically called Broken Heart Syndrome, a run-in with thyroid cancer, and the loss of both parents.

These experiences led Cynthia to commit to becoming more present, embodied, and connected with the natural world, while delving deeper into the experience of oneness she has glimpsed throughout her life.

To contact the Author
please email:
LeslieBole@att.com
www.hummingwords.com

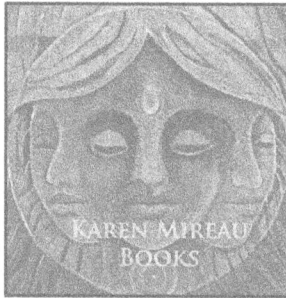

To contact the Publisher
please email:
KarenMireauBooks@gmail.com
www.KarenMireauBooks.com

For Direct Book Orders:
www.Lulu.com